MIX
Papier aus verantwortungsvollen Quellen
Paper from responsible sources
FSC® C105338

Ayoub Loutfi

Interlanguage Pragmatics

A Study of Moroccan EFL Learners' Requests

Anchor Academic
Publishing

Loutfi, Ayoub: Interlanguage Pragmatics: A Study of Moroccan EFL Learners' Requests, Hamburg, Anchor Academic Publishing 2015

Buch-ISBN: 978-3-95489-458-1
PDF-eBook-ISBN: 978-3-95489-958-6
Druck/Herstellung: Anchor Academic Publishing, Hamburg, 2015

Bibliografische Information der Deutschen Nationalbibliothek:
Die Deutsche Nationalbibliothek verzeichnet diese Publikation in der Deutschen Nationalbibliografie; detaillierte bibliografische Daten sind im Internet über http://dnb.d-nb.de abrufbar.

Bibliographical Information of the German National Library:
The German National Library lists this publication in the German National Bibliography. Detailed bibliographic data can be found at: http://dnb.d-nb.de

All rights reserved. This publication may not be reproduced, stored in a retrieval system or transmitted, in any form or by any means, electronic, mechanical, photocopying, recording or otherwise, without the prior permission of the publishers.

Das Werk einschließlich aller seiner Teile ist urheberrechtlich geschützt. Jede Verwertung außerhalb der Grenzen des Urheberrechtsgesetzes ist ohne Zustimmung des Verlages unzulässig und strafbar. Dies gilt insbesondere für Vervielfältigungen, Übersetzungen, Mikroverfilmungen und die Einspeicherung und Bearbeitung in elektronischen Systemen.

Die Wiedergabe von Gebrauchsnamen, Handelsnamen, Warenbezeichnungen usw. in diesem Werk berechtigt auch ohne besondere Kennzeichnung nicht zu der Annahme, dass solche Namen im Sinne der Warenzeichen- und Markenschutz-Gesetzgebung als frei zu betrachten wären und daher von jedermann benutzt werden dürften.

Die Informationen in diesem Werk wurden mit Sorgfalt erarbeitet. Dennoch können Fehler nicht vollständig ausgeschlossen werden und die Diplomica Verlag GmbH, die Autoren oder Übersetzer übernehmen keine juristische Verantwortung oder irgendeine Haftung für evtl. verbliebene fehlerhafte Angaben und deren Folgen.

Alle Rechte vorbehalten

© Anchor Academic Publishing, Imprint der Diplomica Verlag GmbH
Hermannstal 119k, 22119 Hamburg
http://www.diplomica-verlag.de, Hamburg 2015
Printed in Germany

ABSTRACT

Interlanguage Pragmatics: A Study of Moroccan EFL Learners' Requests

By

Ayoub Loutfi

The ultimate goal of this study is to investigate the issue of pragmatic transfer from L1 into the interlanguage of Moroccan learners of English, namely when these learners make requests in English. More specifically, this study seeks to compare the average frequencies of direct and indirect strategies used by both native Moroccan English as a foreign language learners and native English speakers. Finally, this study will further attempt to explore whether transfer decreases as the study level increases, namely the case of the Moroccan EFL university learners at the first and the third level of University.

A number of sixty subjects take part in the present study. They are divided into two groups. The first group involves the Moroccan learners of English who in turn bifurcated into two groups of academic level: Second Year (N=20) and Third year (N=20). The subjects in the second group are 20 native speakers of English. In order to answer the research questions addressed in this study, the Discourse Completion Task (DCT) is adopted. This DCT provides the subjects with a number of seven situations in which different situations are controlled, namely social distance, power relation, and the degree of imposition. A Moroccan Arabic DCT is also used in order to examine how Moroccan students perform requests in their mother tongues.

The results reveal that evidence of pragmatic transfer is found in the requests produced by Moroccan learners of English. Thus, the first hypothesis is confirmed. The second finding is that academic level does not play a major role in pragmatic ability. For this fact, the second research hypothesis is rejected in favor of the null hypothesis drawing the conclusion that pragmatic transfer is not related to academic level. To sum up the whole, a number of research and pedagogical implications are suggested.

DEDICATION

To the memory of my grandfather,
May his soul rest in peace!

To my parents and my two sisters whose very moral and financial support I have always appreciated.

ACKNOWLEDGEMENTS

There are many people who helped me to write this piece of study. First and foremost, I am greatly indebted to Professor Nourddine Amrous for his guiding and assisting at all stages of this work and for supplying necessary materials and documents. I owe a great debt of gratitude to the participants in this study for their outstanding cooperation and willingness to share their thoughts with me. For help and generous support I should thank Mr. Adil Azhar and Prof. Iqbal Zeddari.

I am also grateful to those friends who helped me to collect data for the study. In this respect, I thank Hicham Ahamdi, Youssef Frej, and Othman Maghnaoui. I am subsequently indebted to my seminar classmates whose discussions and interest have been a source of motivation that keeps me going.

Last, but far from least, my very sincere thanks go to my parents, sisters, and my uncle Aziz for their moral and financial support. In fact, there are too many people to enumerate that some of whom were undeservedly omitted. Of course, however, I am responsible for any shortcomings in the study; any credit I happily share it with all mentioned above.

TABLE OF CONTENTS

ABSTRACT 7
DEDICATION 9
ACKNOWLEDGEMENTS 11
LIST OF ABBREVIATIONS 15
GENERAL INTRODUCTION 17
    I.1   Objectives and Rational 17
    I.2   Why Requests? 18
    I.4   Research Questions and Hypothesis: 18
    I.5   Organization of the Study 19

CHAPTER ONE
REVIEW OF THE LITERATURE 20
    II.1   Introduction 20
    II.2   The Theoretical Background 20
        II.2.1   Pragmatic competence 20
        II.2.2   Speech Acts 21
        II.2.3   Cross-cultural Pragmatics: 23
        II.2.4   Interlanguage Pragmatics 24
    II.3   Pragmatic Transfer 24
        II.3.1   On Transfer 24
        II.3.2   Pragmalinguistic/Sociopragmatic Transfer 25
    II.4   Defining Requests 25
        II.4.1   Direct and Indirect Strategies 26
        II.4.2   The two types of indirect strategies 26
            II.4.2.1   Conventionally indirect strategies 26
            II.4.2.2   Non-conventionally Indirect Strategies (Hints) 27
        II.4.3   Modification Categories 27
        II.4.4   Previous Studies in the Moroccan Context 28
    II.5   Conclusion 29

CHAPTER TWO
METHODOLOGY 30
    III.1 Introduction 30
    III.2 Research Questions and Hypothesis: 30

    III.2.1 Research Questions: 30
    III.2.1 Research Hypothesis: 31
  III.3 Subjects 31
    III.3.1 Proficiency Level and Academic Background 33
  III.4 Research instrument 34
    III.4.1 The discourse completion task 34
    III.4.2 Description and Rationale 34
    III.4.3 Situational Variables 35
    III.4.4 The Moroccan Arabic DCT 36
  III.5 Data Collection Procedures: 36
    III.5.1 Data analysis 36
  III.6 Conclusion 37

CHAPTER THREE
RESULTS & DISCUSSION 38
  IV.1 Introduction 38
  IV.2 Pragmalinguistic Analysis 38
    IV.2.1 Major Request strategies by NSs and Mlrs 39
    IV.2.2 Interlanguage Pragmalinguistic Transfer in the Use of the Major Strategies 39
  IV.3 Request Sub-strategies used by NSs and MLrs 41
    IV.3.1 Directness 41
      IV.3.1.1 Direct strategies 41
      IV.3.1.2 Directness used by MLrs 42
      IV.3.1.3 Conventionally indirect strategies (CISs) 43
      IV.3.1.4 Perspectives: 45
  IV.4 Sociopragmatic Analysis 47
    IV.4.1 Directness 48
    IV.4.2 Perspectives 51
  IV.5 Conclusion 53

GENERAL CONCLUSION 54
  V.1 Summary of the objectives 54
  V.2 Summary of the Methodology 54
  V.3 Summary of the Results 54

REFERENCES 57

LIST OF ABBREVIATIONS

CA:	Contrastive Analysis.
CAH:	Contrastive Analysis Hypothesis.
CCSARP:	Cross Cultural Speech Act Realization Project.
CISs:	Conventionally Indirect Strategies.
DCT:	Discourse Completion Test.
EFL:	English as a Foreign Language.
HD:	Hearer-Dominance.
IL:	Interlanguage.
ILP:	Interlanguage Pragmatics.
L1:	First Language.
L2:	Second Language.
MLrs:	Moroccan Learners of English.
MLrs1:	First Year Moroccan Learners.
MLrs3:	Third Year Moroccan Learners.
NSs:	Native Speakers.
SD:	Speaker-Dominance.
SLA:	Second Language Acquisition.

GENERAL INTRODUCTION

I.1 Objectives and Rational

The way language is acquired and learnt has for long been an intriguing issue in social science. This question has attracted researchers from a variety of disciplines and from different theoretical persuasion and predilections. The process of second language acquisition[1] is yet another of area that is worthy of investigation, given to the agglomerate of the issues that this process engenders to second language learners (L2, henceforth). Of interest to the present study is the way this process jointly interacts with a number of factors, most important of which is the learner's mother tongue.

In this regard, a question of considerable interest is whether or not a learner's first language affects the process of second language acquisition, insofar as this interference may either help ease or thwart the developmental path of the learning process. Another interesting query concerns the extent of which formal education reduces or helps circumvent this interference.

On this view, the present study sets as its research goals the objectives of providing an investigation of the issue of pragmatic transfer from L1 into the interlanguage of Moroccan learners of English, namely when these learners make requests in English. More specifically, this study will seek to compare the average frequencies of direct and indirect strategies used by both native Moroccan English as a foreign language learners and native speakers of English. Finally, this study will further attempt to explore whether transfer decreases as the study level increases, namely the case of the Moroccan EFL university learners at the first and the third level of university.

This being said, the impetus for conducting this research within the area of Interlanguage Pragmatics stems from a variety of factors. Firstly, there are aspects in which the role of socio-cultural rules and pragmatics cannot go unnoticed, the lack of which results in communication breakdown (see for examples Wang (2004) and Lin (2008)). Important though grammatical competence may seem, there are cases in which socio-cultural rules transcend grammatical rules (Hymes, 1971). Secondly, I have selected this topic to know how L2, namely Moroccan ones, perform the speech act of request in both their L1 and L2, and what influences the former exerts on the latter, in this case English. Equally importantly, there is an

---

[1] Throughout this study, the term second language will be used in the sense of the languages acquired/learnt other than one's mother tongue, be they second, third, fourth...etc.

ostensibly scanty number of research that have been conducted in Interlanguage Pragmatics, namely within the Moroccan context; hence, many questions still remain uncovered and a lack of an in-depth understanding of the factors that influence interlanguage pragmatic development is yet to be revealed.

I.2   Why Requests?

The speech act of request has been chosen in the present study as the best tool through which one can identify about Interlanguage Pragmatic transfer. Indeed, requests are used in every-day communication in both Moroccan Arabic and English and, therefore, they occur in a variety of forms (e.g. imperatives, declaratives and interrogatives) with differing situational features under different social parameters. Furthermore, a request constitutes a face-threatening act (Brown and Levinson 1978; 1987); hence, speakers will need to make use of varying strategies so as to reduce the threat and to decrease the potential damage. Last but not least, there have been studies that have been undertaken in the illocutionary act of requests. Therefore, there is a firm ground upon which one can base further study.

I.4   Research Questions and Hypothesis:

Research Questions:

This study seeks to examine the use of L2 speech act of request by Moroccan learners of English. Under this light, the purpose is to explore the strategies used by Moroccan learners of English and to see the amount of transfer from L1 to L2 when they perform requests in English. To this end, this study will intend to answer the following questions:

1. To what extent do Moroccan learners of English rely on their L1 in the production of English requests?

2. To what extent does the level of proficiency affect Moroccan learners" production of English requests?

3. To what extent do Moroccans learners differ with English native speakers in the production of English requests?

Research Hypothesis:

In pursuance of this aim, two hypotheses have been formulated:

Hypothesis 1: There is evidence of pragmatic transfer in the English requests produced by Moroccan learners of English.

Hypothesis 2: Pragmatic transfer decreases as the study level increases.

I.5 Organization of the Study

The present study is made up of four chapters organized as follows. The first chapter will seek to define some key-concepts so as to situate the present study in its theoretical background. This section also reviews the most important studies that have been undertaken in Morocco within the frames of Interlanguage Pragmatics. The second chapter intends to give and present a rigorous description whereby the data was collected. The third chapter falls into two parts. The first reveals the results of the data collection and the other one will lay the ground for the discussion of these results. The study then will be closed with a general conclusion, drawing some research and pedagogical implications.

Chapter One
Review of the Literature

II.1 Introduction

The aim of this chapter is to situate the present study in its theoretical perspectives under which the findings are meant to be discussed. The chapter is introduced with a discussion of the pragmatic component in linguistics, particularly as part of the native speakers" communicative competence. Moreover, the chapter briefly traces the major pragmatics trends within the frames of speech act theory. Next, an overview is given of the fields of cross-cultural pragmatics and interlanguage. A definition is supplied of the field of interlanguage pragmatics, to which this study belongs, along with a concise description of some relevant studies carried out in the Moroccan context.

II.2 The Theoretical Background

II.2.1 Pragmatic competence

The concept of communicative competence was first introduced by the anthropologist and sociolinguist Hymes (1964) to refer to communicative competence that does not consist only of grammatical competence; that is to say, not only should linguistic competence involve the formal knowledge of the target language, but also the knowledge of the sociocultural rules of appropriate language use. The fact of the matter is that Hymes" concept of competence was introduced as a reaction against Chomsky's (1965) notion of competence. For Chomsky, competence encompasses the perfect knowledge of an ideal-speaker listener in a homogeneous speech community. As Chomsky (1965: 3) states:

> "Linguistic theory is concerned primarily with an ideal speaker-listener in a completely homogeneous speech community, who knows its language perfectly, and is unaffected by such grammatically irrelevant conditions as memory limitations, distractions, shifts of attention and errors in applying this knowledge of the language in actual performance."

In this regard, Hymes (1971) maintains that „there are rules of use without which the rules of grammar would be useless (1971: 278). As a matter of fact, Hymes" concept of communicative competence brought a radical shift to the study of language, which began to account for studying language in its actual use that is appropriate and acceptable to a particular speech community. More recently, other linguists have extended the idea of communicative competence further. In this regard, Canale and Swain (1983) include three components within their model of communicative competence

The sociolinguistic component which addresses the extent to which an utterance produced is accepted and appropriate to a particular socially and culturally defined setting. In addition to the sociolinguistic component, Canal and Swain's model of communication competence also include the discourse and strategic competence[2].

It is along these lines that Bachman (1990) emphasized the role of pragmatics in communicative competence. Pragmatic competence is concerned with the ability that enables speakers to produce and understand utterances in relation to specific communication purposes and specific speech context in order to produce effective communication. Bachman subdivided pragmatic competence into illocutionary competence and sociolinguistic competence. The former is described as the knowledge of communicative strategies and how to use them appropriately. The sociolinguistic competence, on the other hand, deals with the acceptable use of a particular language within a particular context.

The British pragmatician Leech (1983) subdivided pragmatic competence into pragmalinguistics and sociopragmatics. Pragmalinguistics can be applied to the more linguistic end of pragmatics- where we consider the particular resources which a given language provides for conveying particular illocutions (Leech, 1983: 11). In this regard, Kasper (1997) elucidates that such resources are the strategies for performing speech acts that include directness and indirectness strategies and linguistic forms, which can alleviate or intensify speech acts.

Sociopragmatics, on the other hand, can be better defined in Leech's terms as "the sociological interface of pragmatics" (Leech, 1983: 10). It is concerned then with the interface of linguistic action and social structure. More specifically, it demonstrates the effect of such limitation as social status, social distance and degree of imposition on the choice of linguistic realization of a particular communicative acts and strategies.

II.2.2 Speech Acts

Speech act theory can be traced back from the work of the two philosophers John Austin (1962) and John Searle (1969; 1975; 1976). The core of this theory is that speakers perform illocutionary acts by producing utterances. An illocutionary act is a particular language function performed by utterances. That is to say, through the utterances a given speaker uses,

---

[2] See Canal and Swain (1983) for more details.

s/he performs an act which s/he intends to have an effect on her/his interlocutor. As Searle (1980, p. vii) puts it:

> "The minimal unit of communication is not a sentence or other expression, but rather the performance of certain kinds of acts, such as making statements, asking questions, giving orders, describing... etc."

According to Austin, every speech act consists of three elements: the locutionary act, the illocutionary act, and the perlocutionary act.

1. **The Locutionary Act** is the act of uttering something with a certain literal or linguistic meaning.

2. **The Illocutionary Act** is the speaker's intention that is realized in producing an utterance, such as informing, requesting, ordering, etc.

3. **The Perlocutionary Act** is the intended effect the speaker wants to achieve and to have effect on the hearer, e.g. to convince him, to persuade him, etc.

Building on Austin's work, Searle proposed an alternative classification which is briefly detailed in the following five classes of speech act, namely:

Representatives/Assertives: Speaker commits him/herself to the belief that the propositional content of the utterance is true.

Directives: is the attempt of the speaker to get the interlocutor to do something.

Commissives: Speaker commits him/herself to a future course of action.

Expressives: Speaker expresses his/her psychological attitude towards some prior action or state of affairs.

Declarations: Speaker brings about a correspondence between the propositional content and the world; institutionally-bound.

Following Austin and Searle, a large number of studies have been undertaken in both cross-cultural and interlanguage pragmatics within the frames of the speech acts and their various aspects, namely in the context of second and foreign language learning. Accordingly, such studies paved the way to the emergence of new fields of inquiry, particularly cross-cultural pragmatics and interlanguage pragmatics.

II.2.3 Cross-cultural Pragmatics:

Cross-cultural pragmatics has been defined as a field of inquiry which compares the ways in which two or more languages are used in communication. The field is an important new branch of contrastive linguistic studies because in any two languages different features of the social context may be found to be relevant in deciding what can be expressed and how it is conventionally expressed. (House-Edmondson 1986: 282).

Typically, the way interlocutors successfully sustain conversation with one another has always been a concern of a number of pragmaticians. Indeed, their assumption is that people adhere to certain principles so as to succeed in sustaining a conversation. One such principle is the Cooperative Principle[3] which supposes that interactants cooperate in the conversation by contributing to speech event (Grice, 1975). Another principle (Leech, 1983) is that of interlocutors behave politely to one another and respect each other's face (Brown and Levinson, 1987).

A number of studies, however, reported that what is believed to be polite in one language may sometimes not be polite in another due to cultural differences. (Wierzbicka 1985, in Blum-Kulka, House, and Kasper, 1989).

The Cross-Cultural Speech Act Realization Project (henceforth CCSARP) is the most notable research project in the area of cross-cultural pragmatics and interlanguage pragmatics. It aimed at establishing patterns of speech act realization under different social contexts across various languages and cultures using a single coding system. (Blum-Kulka, House and Kasper (1989: 22). The data of the CCSARP were collected through the use of the discourse completion task (DCT) and the varieties analyzed included American English, Australian English, British English, Canadian French, Danish, German, Hebrew and Argentinean Spanish.

Blum-Kulka, House, and Kasper (1989) in their book, Cross-cultural Pragmatics: Requests and Apologies, reported nine studies undertaken within the CCSARP. Five of these studies dealt with requests, three with apologies, and only one with methodological problems faced in the study of requests and apologies. For requests, which is the main concern and of direct relevance to the present study, Blum-Kulka investigated the role of conventional indirectness, Weizman focused on hints, House examined the functions of politeness marker „please" in both English and German, and Blum-Kulka and House identified the relationship between the realization patterns

---

[3] Basically, the cooperative Principle or the so called Gricean maxims is made up of four maxims. Obeying these maxims yield an effective communication. (For more details see Grice (1975).

and the perception of situational factors in five languages. In the last study, Faerch and Kasper approached the issues of modification in interlanguage requesting productions.

II.2.4 Interlanguage Pragmatics

Interlanguage pragmatics is a quickly developing branch of SLA research. Over the last two decades, a number of studies have been undertaken in the area of interlanguage pragmatics (Ellis, 1994; Kasper & Dahl, 1991; Kasper & Rose, 1999; and Thomas, among so many others). Now this field of inquiry is considered as a separate field of research. The bulk of the studies have predominantly been to identify the ways in which and the extent to which non-native learners of a second language use illocutionary acts differently from native speakers of the target language. However, the scope of interlanguage pragmatics has been restricted by a number of researchers (Kasper and Dahl 1991) to be particularly concerned with speech acts. In this respect, this area of research has come mainly to refer to "the study of nonnative speakers" comprehension, production, and acquisition of linguistic action in L2, or, put briefly, ILP investigates, how to do things with words" in a second language" (Kasper 1998b: 184). However, ILP also includes studies addressing conversational management, discourse organization, or sociolinguistic aspects of language use such as choice of address forms will be outside the scope of this study.

Kasper and Schmidt (1996) argue that the field of interlanguage pragmatics is basically modeled on cross-cultural pragmatics. The studies that have been conducted are essentially interested in identifying the influence of learners" native language and culture on their L2 or FL speech act performance. These studies maintain that pragmatic transfer plays an important role in cross-cultural miscommunication.

II.3 Pragmatic Transfer

II.3.1 On Transfer

The emergence of transfer as a phenomenon in SLA is more often than not associated with the Contrastive Analysis (CA), which was related to the behaviorists view of language learning and to structural linguistics. They claim that under the most of the difficulties confronting the L2 learners were imposed by their L1. The Contrastive Analysis Hypothesis (CAH) points out that structurally different language would result in the production of errors, which affect the process of the acquisition of the L2. In fact, Sharwood-Smith and Kellerman (1986: 1) suggest restricting the scope of the term to "those processes that lead to the incorporation of elements from one language into another", arguing that the notion of transfer is inadequate and, therefore, posit an umbrella term, cross-linguistic influence, that allows "to subsume under one heading such phenomenon as transfer, interference, avoidance, borrowing and L2-related aspects of language loss. However, researchers such Odlin (1989) or Ellis (1994) defines transfer as:

> "Transfer is to be seen as a general cover term for a number of different kinds of influence from languages other than the L2. The study of transfer involves the study of errors (negative transfer), facilitation (positive transfer) avoidance of target language forms, and their over-use" (Ellis, 1994: 341).

II.3.2 Pragmalinguistic/Sociopragmatic Transfer

Thomas (1983: 99) differentiates between two types of pragmatic transfer, namely pragmalinguistic and sociopragmatic transfer. In this light, Gabriele Kasper (1992) suggested a more comprehensive definition. She describes pragmalinguistic transfer as

> "The process whereby the illocutionary force or politeness value assigned to particular linguistic material in L1 influences learners' perception and production of form-function mappings in L2". (Kasper 1992: 209)

In this regard, pragmalinguistic transfer refers to when learners select certain strategies and norms from their L1 to transport into their interlanguage. The transported items affect the illocutionary force or relative politeness value of a particular utterance in a manner which may be different from that of the target norms.

Sociopragmatic transfer, on the other hand, is described as:

> "The influence of the social perceptions underlying language users' interpretation and performance of linguistic action in L1 on their assessment of subjectively equivalent L2 contexts. (Kasper Odense postgraduate seminar 1998, cf. also Kasper 1992: 209).

All things concerned, pragmatic transfer is defined as the influence exerted by learners" pragmatic knowledge of languages and cultures other than L2 on their comprehension, production and learning of L2 pragmatic information. (Kasper 1992: 207).

II.4 Defining Requests

Requests as speech acts have been defined from many perspectives. Indeed, Blum-kulka (1991: 256) defines requests as "pre-event acts, intended to affect the hearer's behavior". In the same vein, Becker (1982: 1) defines requests as an utterance that is intended to indicate the speaker's desire to regulate the behavior of the listener – that is, to get the listener to do something. Requests are linked to a number of interactional, illocutionary and sociolinguistic characteristics (Ellis, 1994: 176-8).

At the interactional level, requests are seen to be as discourse initiators in the sense they are meant to have the hearer to perform an action. At the illocutionary level, there three conditions that requires the speaker to obey for the requests to be appropriate. First, the speaker must be sincere in his or her wish that the hearer perform the act. Second, the speaker believes that the hearer is able to perform the act. Third, the speaker does not believe that the act will be performed without the request (Ellis, 1994: 167).

This being said, a given request can be performed at different levels of directness, namely direct strategies, conventionally indirect strategies and non-conventionally indirect strategies.

II.4.1 Direct and Indirect Strategies

Direct strategies, just as the name implies, are defined as utterances in which the propositional content (sentence meaning) of the utterance is consistent with the speaker's intent (speaker meaning) (Holtgraves, 1986). That is, when the speaker intends to make a request, s /he makes it in an apparent way. Indirect strategies, on the other hand, are utterances in which the speaker's meaning and the propositional content are not the same. Indirect strategies, therefore, imply more than one meaning or illocutionary force, while direct strategies communicate only one meaning or requestive act. In fact, indirect strategies are generally believed to be used for the sake of politeness (Brown & Levinson, 1978; 1987; H. Clark, 1979; H. Clark & Schunk, 1980; R. Lakoff, 1973; Leech, 1983; Searle, 1975). Furthermore, Searle (1975: 64) points out that politeness is the chief motivation for indirectness". In a similar vein, Leech (1983: 108) maintains that indirect strategies tend to be more polite because of their optionality. However, indirect strategies are not always considered to be polite when they are not used in their appropriate context.

II.4.2 The two types of indirect strategies

II.4.2.1 Conventionally indirect strategies

In an attempt to define conventional indirectness Searle (1975: 76) states that:

> "there can be conventions of usage....I am suggesting that can you, could you, I want you to, and numerous other forms are conventional ways of making requests,...but at the same time they do not have an imperative meaning"

Conventions of usage are, according to H.Clark (1979), the amalgamation of conventions of means and conventions of forms. Conventions of means are sentences that are meant to perform an indirect request. Indeed, they are used to question the hearer's ability. Conventions of form, on the other hand, specify the exact wording used for a given indirect request. For example, "Can you close the window?" or "Could you close the door?"

II.4.2.2 Non-conventionally Indirect Strategies (Hints)

Non-conventionally indirect strategies are generally seen as the requestive acts that can take any linguistic form or hints. That is to say, requestive hints allow many illocutionary goals as the contexts suggest. More specifically, Blum-Kulka (1989: 42) defines non-conventionally indirect strategies as follows:

> *"For conventional indirectness, conventions of propositional content (means) and linguistic form combine to signal requestive force. Non-conventionally indirectness, on the other hand, is in principle open-ended, both in terms of propositional content and linguistic form as well as pragmatic force. Thus, there are no limitations."*

In the quote above, it is clear that in using that strategy a speaker can deny or avoid his or her intention or responsibility of making a request. (Brown & Levinson, 1978; 1987). Another benefit in favor of this strategy is that the speaker can satisfy negative face to a degree greater than that afforded by the negative politeness strategy. (Brown & Levinson, 1987: 73). However polite such strategy might be, it can be inappropriate in some particular context. By way of illustration, a study was conducted by Blum-Kulka (1987) revealed that native speakers of Hebrew and American-English perceived conventionally indirect strategies to be more polite than hints in the sense that they lack pragmatic clarity. In addition, non-conventionally indirect strategies are considered to be ambiguous because they can carry multiple pragmatic forces (Blum-Kulka, 1983; Weizman, 1989; 1993). For example, the sentence "it' cold in here" carries more than one meaning which again depends on the context.

II.4.3 Modification Categories

Modification categories are strategies used by a speaker to vary the impact of a request. Indeed, they are linguistic elements whose function is to modulate the impact of a request mitigators, reinforcers or aggravators. Fraser (1978: 13) defines mitigators as elements that soften or ease the force of the request intentionally. Reinforcers are used to increase the force of the request. Aggravators are elements that modulate the request in the opposite direction of mitigation such as threats, insults, and moralizing statements (Blum-Kulka, 1982: 35).

In addition, there are two types of modifications, namely external and internal modification categories. To begin with, external modification categories can either occur after the request:

head act + supportive move, or they can precede the request: supportive move + head act. Internal modification categories, on the other hand, are divided in two categories. The first category is "downgraders". They are elements used to mitigate the impositive force of a request. For example, when a speaker add the element "please" to a request as a signal of politeness. The second category includes "upgrades" that emphasize the degree of coerciveness such as the use of intensifiers, commitment indicators, and time intensifiers.

II.4.4 Previous Studies in the Moroccan Context

Requests, among other speech acts, have been a subject matter for many researchers, particularly those interested in second language teaching and learning. Indeed, numerous studies conducted so far have investigated the production, comprehension or perception of requests by L2 or FL learners (Blum-Kulka, 1982; Blum-Kulka & Olshtain, 1984; Blum-Kulka, 1987; Blum-Kulka et al., 1989), to cite but a few. Yet there are an ostensibly scanty number of studies on interlanguage pragmatics among Moroccan EFL learners. More recently, however, two studies have been undertaken in Morocco that dealt with the issue of interlanguage pragmatics. First of these is Latif (2001) and the second study is Benbarka (2002). The focus of

Latif"s study was to investigate how Moroccan learners of English realized the speech act of requesting. The objectives of the study were concerned with tapping Moroccan learners" underlying perceptions of some contextual variables in order, first, to contrast them with native speakers" and, second, to examine the effect of such perceptions on requesting performance.

The results revealed that Moroccan learners use more direct strategies and modification categories than native speakers. Latif (2002) also pointed out that fourth year Moroccan learners showed more directness, verbosity and syntactic proficiency than their first year counterparts.

The second study was conducted by Benbarka (2002) of Benbarka"s study where the focus was to investigate the development of pragmatic ability in Moroccan learners of English. More specifically, it aimed at examining the relationship between pragmatic transfer and foreign language proficiency with a particular focus on speech act of apology.

The result showed that pragmatic transfer from the native language exists in the English apologies produced by Moroccan learners of English. Moreover, her study demonstrated that pragmatic transfer decreases as learners become proficient in the target language.

II.5 Conclusion

This chapter has attempted to briefly and concisely delineate the theoretical foundation from which the study is reviewed. The first part traced the major issues debated in the fields of cross-cultural pragmatics and IL pragmatics. A number of key concepts were defined and discussed. Among the notions which were explained in this chapter are terms such as pragmatic competence, speech acts theory, cross-cultural pragmatics, interlanguage pragmatics, pragmatic transfer, pragmalinguistic/sociopragmatic transfer, and requests. The last section focused on the previous studies undertaken in Morocco on the production of speech acts, namely apology and request. The next chapter will be concerned with outlining the methodological procedures and measures followed in the present investigation.

Chapter Two
Methodology

III.1 Introduction

The present study endeavors to investigate the issue of pragmatic transfer from L1 into the interlanguage of Moroccan learners of English, namely when they make requests in English. More specifically, this study will seek to compare the average frequencies of direct and indirect strategies used by both native Moroccan English as a foreign language learners and native speakers of English. Besides, this study will further attempt to explore whether transfer decreases as the study level increased, the case of the Moroccan EFL university learners: The first and the third level of university. In order to situate the study in its theoretical perspectives, some of the relevant literature pertinent to the issue was reviewed. The aim of the present chapter then is to describe and discuss the methodology of data collection and analysis. For this fact, the different sections will demonstrate information relative to research instrument (i.e. the Discourse Completion Task (DCT), the rationale behind choosing this instrument, subjects, the procedures, and the statistical tools for data analysis.

III.2 Research Questions and Hypothesis:

III.2.1 Research Questions:

This study seeks to examine the use of L2 speech act of request by Moroccan learners of English. Under this light, the purpose is to explore the strategies used by Moroccan learners of English and to see the amount of transfer from L1 into L2 when they perform requests in English. To this end, this study will intend to answer the following questions:

1. To what extent do Moroccan learners of English rely on their L1 in the production of English requests?

2. To what extent does the level of proficiency affect Moroccan learners" production of English requests?

3. To what extent do Moroccans learners differ with English native speakers in the production of English requests?

III.2.1 Research Hypothesis:

In pursuance of this aim, two hypotheses have been formulated:

Hypothesis 1: There is evidence of pragmatic transfer in the English requests produced by Moroccan learners of English.

Hypothesis 2: Pragmatic transfer decreases as the study level increases.

III.3 Subjects

The number of subjects having taken part in the present study totaled 56 subjects. They were divided into two groups. The first group comprises the Moroccan learners of English who in turn bifurcated into two groups of academic level: Second Year (N=20) and Third year (N=20). The subjects in the second group are 20 native speakers of English. The choice of these two groups is justified by the fact that the main focus of the study is to compare the average frequencies of direct and indirect strategies used by both native Moroccan English as a foreign language learners and native English speaker when they make request in English and, indeed, to test the hypothesis that transfer decreases as the study level increases.

The sample of the Moroccan learners of English includes both male and female subjects, whose age ranges from 18 to 24. All of these subjects are students at the English Department at the faculty of Letters-Rabat. The other group of native speakers was Americans native speakers. Some of whom were teachers at AMIDEST; others were just volunteers who showed their great willingness to take part in this research.

The tables below show the Moroccan learners and native speakers" distribution according to age and gender.

Table 1: Distribution of 1st year students according to age and gender

First Year Students			
Age Section	Males	Females	Total
18-21	9	10	19
22-24	1	0	1
Total	10	10	20

Table 2: Distribution of 3rd year students according to age and gender

Third Year Students			
Age Section	Males	Females	Total
19-21	3	11	14
22-24	3	2	5
Above 25	1	0	1
Total	7	13	20

Table 3: Distribution of American Native Speakers according to age and gender

Native Speakers			
Age Section	Males	Females	Total
19-21	1	4	5
22-24	1	1	1
Above 25	5	6	13
Total	7	11	20

Noteworthy is that in this study, variables such as age, gender need not to be taken into account, insofar as the purpose of the study is to explore the phenomenon of transfer in EFL context. In fact, the subjects are selected on the basis of their level of proficiency.

III.3.1 Proficiency Level and Academic Background

Before delving into describing proficiency level of the subjects, it should be pointed out that defining language proficiency per se seems to be problematic in the sense that academic level is not always related to language proficiency. For instance, a student whose academic level is high may or may not be proficient in using the language. Therefore, it was assumed that the subjects should perceive a proficiency test which the present study could not afford. All these, among so many other things, constitute the limitations of the present study.

The first year group is introduced to the basics of English, namely Grammar, Reading comprehension, and Spoken English, a course which tries to improve their oral communication and communicative behavior.

Concerning the subjects from the Third group, they are assumed to be more fluent users of the English language. Given the nature of the courses they attended which require them to have a good mastery of the language as well as they are asked to submit a whole monograph in partial fulfillment of the BA degree.

III.4 Research instrument

III.4.1 The discourse completion task

The most commonly used data collection in the field of cross-cultural and Interlanguage Pragmatics is the Discourse Completion Test (henceforth DCT). A DCT was first developed by Blum-kulka (1982) for her study of speech acts. Subsequently, it was adopted by a large number of researchers by virtue of the fact that it enables them to gather large amounts of data in a set amount of time. Furthermore, it allows researchers to control a variety of the situations such as social distance, social status in order to assess the speech act being studied, and to compare the results between two language speakers, namely native speakers and second language learners. As a matter of fact, Beebe (1985: 10, in Wolfson et al. 1989) points out that the DCT is a reliable tool for:

- Creating an initial classification of semantic formulas and strategies that will occur in natural speech.

- Studying the stereotypical perceived requirements for a socially appropriate response.

- Gaining insight into social and psychological factors that are likely to affect speech and performance.

- Ascertaining the canonical shape of refusals, apologies……in the minds of the speakers of that language.

However, one should note that every data collection technique has its own advantages and drawbacks. In this respect, Brown and Levinson (1987) demonstrate that what people claim they would say in the hypothetical situation is not necessarily what they actually say in the real situation. Hence, many participants may not respond spontaneously as in natural situation because they have time to think and prepare to the situations. Besides, some non-native students have a limited set of vocabulary and, therefore, they tend to use only the words they are familiar with.

To wind up, DCT is still considered the most widely used instrument in the field of ILP and cross-cultural pragmatics.

III.4.2 Description and Rationale

The DCT that was administered to the subjects who participated in this study consists of seven situations. Each situation is accompanied with a brief description of the participants, their role relationship, and the request goal. The subjects were asked to respond spontaneously to these situations and write down what they would say. They were given a blank space in which they had to provide their request. The purpose was to assess the various requestive strategies used by both native Moroccan English as a foreign language learners and native English speakers.

The choice of such an instrument can be justified by dint of its popularity among researchers in the field of ILP and cross-cultural pragmatics. Besides, it allows providing a variety of situations that natural setting may not provide in a limited amount of time.

III.4.3 Situational Variables

As mentioned before, the DCT used in this study consists of seven situations, each of which varies in terms of power, distance, the degree of imposition, and the request goal. The following table summarizes these specifications:

Table 4: Situational Variables Controlled on the DCT

Situation	Power	Distance	Imposition	Request goal
1. Borrowing	=P	+D	-IM	B
2. Parking	+P	-D	+IM	A
3. Kitchen	=P	+D	-IM	A
4. Student to Professor	-P	+D	+IM	B
5. Permission	-P	+D	-IM	C
6. Manager to Employee	+P	+D	+IM	A
7. Book	=P	-D	+IM	B

+P: High Power, =P: Equal Power, -P: Less Power, +D: Familiar, -D: Unfamiliar, +IM: High Imposition, -IM: Low Imposition, A: Right/ Duty, B: Favor/Service, C: Permission.

III.4.4 The Moroccan Arabic DCT

Moroccan Arabic DCT was used in order to examine how Moroccan students perform requests in their mother tongues and also to see whether there is pragmatic transfer in the English requests produced by Moroccan learners of English. The whole seven situations were identical to that of English in terms of participants: the same role, and the same setting. In fact, the same procedures were taken into account, namely the social distance and social status.

III.5 Data Collection Procedures:

The data was collected in May 2011. At such a time, exams were drawing near; hence, it was difficult to administer the questionnaire to all the Moroccan subject at once. For this fact, the DCT was given to them in small groups of three of five students at a time. First, the students were asked to read the situations carefully before they respond. No sooner had they finished the DCT than they were given the Moroccan Arabic version of the questionnaire.

Concerning native speakers" subjects, the majority of them had hectic schedules; it was difficult to administer the questionnaire to them collectively. As a solution, they were given the questionnaire and collected it back when they had filled it.

It should be noted that both Moroccan and native speakers" subjects were encouraged to respond to the situations spontaneously as in natural situations. Indeed, no time limit was set.

III.5.1 Data analysis

Following previous studies in the field of ILP, the present study adopts the coding scheme used in the CCSARP coding categories (Blum-Kulka, House, Kasper 1989) by dint of its popularity along with its credibility by virtue of its adaptation by a great number of speech act project. The analysis of the Moroccan EFL learners" realization of request will be based on request realization strategies and perspectives. Indeed, in an attempt to analyze the data, a number of techniques were adopted, namely the frequency analyses whereby the different strategies will be described across groups. The strategy types are presented in Table 5.

Table 5: Request strategy types: Definitions and examples

Types and their definitions	Examples
Direct Strategies	
1. Mood derivable The grammatical mood of the verb signals the illocutionary force of the request. The imperative is the prototypical form. Elliptical imperative structures express the same directness level.	Stop making that noise.
2. Obligation statements The utterance states the obligation of the addressee to carry out the act.	You have to move you car
3. Want statement The utterance states the speaker's personal need or desire that the addressees carry out the act.	I want you to lend me you new suit.
Conventionally indirect strategies	
4. Suggestory formulae The utterance contains a suggestion to do something.	Why don't you clean the kitchen?
5. Query preparatory The utterance contains reference to preparatory conditions for the feasibility of the request (e.g. ability, willingness, or the possibility of the act being performed). The speaker questions the presence of the chosen preparatory condition.	Could you please postpone the exam?
Nonconventionally indirect strategies The utterance makes no reference or only partial reference to the object or element needed for implementation of the act.	You have left the kitchen in a right mess.

III.6 Conclusion

This chapter has brought into focus the discussion of the elements involved in the process of collecting the data. Besides, the chapter provided a presentation of the research subjects, along with a description of their proficiency level and linguistic background. An attempt has also been made to describe the data analysis and the coding scheme adopted. The next chapter will fall into two parts, one presenting the results of data analysis and the other discussing these results so as to meet the research objectives discussed in the introductory chapter.

Chapter Three
Results & Discussion

IV.1 Introduction

The previous chapter was devoted to describing the measures by which the data will be analyzed. The aim of the present chapter then is to lay the ground for the analysis of these data, along with a discussion of these results so as to answer the research questions addressed in this study. Indeed, this chapter seeks to compare the most used strategies by EFL learners when they perform requests in both English and Moroccan Arabic as compared with native speakers of English. In doing so, it will be easy to examine the issue of transfer as well as to see whether transfer decreases as the study level increases. To this end, transfer will be examined at two levels: Pragmalinguistic and Sociopragmatic level. The former is meant to identify request strategies, perspectives, modifications, and alerters. The sociopragmatics analysis aims to examine the impact of the situational variables such as social distance, power relation, and the degree of imposition on the performance of the speech act of request.

IV.2 Pragmalinguistic Analysis

Pragmalinguistics, as has been defined in the literature, is when learners tend to use certain strategies and norms from their L1 to transport into their interlanguage. The transported items affect the illocutionary force or relative politeness value of a particular utterance in a manner which may be different from that of the target norms. Under this light, this section is concerned with presenting a panoramic view about the major request strategies used by the MLrs1, MLrs3, and NSs.

IV.2.1 Major Request strategies by NSs and Mlrs

Table 6: Frequency and percentage of the major request strategies across the Three Groups.

Group	N	Direct Strategies	Conventionally Indirect Strategies	Hints	Total
NSs	16	18.19*(20)**	72.72(80)	9.09(10)	110
MLrs1	20	33.85 (43)	64.56(82)	1.59(2)	127
MLrs3	20	38.97(53)	57.35(78)	3.68(5)	136
Total	56	100	100	100	373

* Percentages/** Number of strategies.

The results presented in table (1) show that the conventionally indirect strategies were the most widely used, followed by direct strategies. Compared to the other strategies, hints were the leaser used strategies across the three groups. At the first glance, NSs seem to be the least indirect group in the sense that this strategy represents (72.72%), followed by MLrs2 with a percentage of (64.56%). The last group is the MLrs3 with a percentage of (57.35%). Direct strategies, they follow, are the most used by the MLrs. For example, MLrs3 phrased (38.97%) of their request in direct strategies, followed by MLrs1 with (38.97%). NSs, on the other hand, used 18.19% of their requests in direct strategies.

In point of fact, it seems that there are similarities than differences between the three groups in terms of the strategies employed. However, this table also indicates that Mlrs surpass NSs in the use of direct strategies.

IV.2.2 Interlanguage Pragmalinguistic Transfer in the Use of the Major Strategies

The aim of this section is to present the results of the MLrs' performance in both English as an interlanguage (IL) and Moroccan Arabic language in the major requesting strategies.

Table 7: Frequency and percentage of the major request strategies employed by MLrs in their L1 and IL.

	MLrs1				MLrs3			
	English		Moroccan Arabic		English		Moroccan Arabic	
	F	%	F	%	F	%	F	%
Direct Strategies	43	33.85	76	61.41	33	38.97	78	58.22
Conventionally Indirect Strategies	82	64.56	46	34.66	78	57.35	49	36.56
Hints	2	1.59	5	3.93	5	3.68	7	5.22
Total	127	100	127	100	136	100	134	100

Table (7) shows that direct strategies were the most frequently used by MLrs with a percentage that ranges from (58.22%) to (61.41%) in their L1 as compared to their performance in IL. This implies that MLrs" L1 exerts no influence on their performance in the IL of strategies. This claim is justified by the fact that MLrs" performance in the IL is apparently different from that of their L1. Nevertheless, a similar tendency of the use of direct strategies when one compares the use of these strategies in IL. As stated before, Mlrs surpass NSs in the use of direct strategies in the IL. In this regard, one may conclude that there is transfer from L1 into IL in terms of the preference of direct strategies by MLrs in IL as compared to NSs who seem to underuse such strategies.

Another remark that can be made is that hints are the least frequently performed in strategies in both MLrs" L1 and L2. This indicates that the use of hints by MLrs in a similar rate in both L1 and IL may be considered as a positive transfer.

IV.3 Request Sub-strategies used by NSs and MLrs

IV.3.1 Directness

IV.3.1.1 Direct strategies

In order to assess the most used strategies used by the three groups as well as to have a comprehensive and a detailed analysis of the requests performed, this section is concerned with presenting NSs and MLrs" request sub-strategies.

Table 8: Frequency and percentage of Directness across the three groups.

IL sub strategies	NSs		MLrs1		MLrs3	
	F	%	F	%	F	%
Mood derivable	8	38.09	19	41.30	11	28.20
Locution derivable	6	28.75	8	17.39	16	41.02
Want statement	3	14.28	14	30.43	9	23.02
Performatives	2	9.52	5	10.86	3	7.69
Verbless expression	2	9.52	–	–	–	–
Total	21	100	46	100	39	100

The table (3) clearly indicates that mood derivable, locution derivable, and want statement were the most frequently used sub-strategies across the three groups. By way of illustration, the following examples were performed by NSs for these particular strategies:

- This is a no-parking area, please move your car.
- Hey man! You gotta clean the kitchen. That was your party and you left it in a mess.

However, NSs do not heavily rely on direct strategies as the case of MLrs. For the sake of illustration, the following linguistic realizations were employed by MLrs:

- Move your car from here
- You should clean the kitchen
- Clean the mess you and your friend did yesterday.

As shown in the table above, there is an apparent difference between MLrs in the sense that MLrs1 tended to rely heavily on the mood derivable with a percentage of (41.30%), followed by want statement (30.43%). MLrs3, on the other hand, used locution derivable more frequently (41.02%).

It should also be pointed that NSs did not tend to use want statement with a percentage of only (14.28%). This again implies that there is transfer from L1. Indeed, the majority of MLrs opted for performing their want statements with the verb "to want" whereas NSs used the verb "to need". This claim is supported by the fact that MLrs tend to use heavily the verb "to want" in their L1[4]. (Abdou, 2000).

IV.3.1.2 Directness used by MLrs

The present table displays the use of directness by the MLrs in both their L1 and IL. The aim of this analysis is to assess and to identify the similarities and differences in the performance of these strategies in their L1 as well as to examine the issue of transfer between the two groups.

Table 9: Frequency and percentage of Directness employed by MLrs.

	MLrs1				MLrs3			
	English		Arabic		English		Arabic	
	F	%	F	%	F	%	F	%
Mood derivable	19	41.30	46	63.88	11	28.20	55	79.73
Locution derivable	8	17.39	10	13.88	16	41.02	7	10.41
Want statement	14	30.43	16	22.24	9	23.02	3	4.34
Performatives	5	10.86	—	—	3	7.69	4	5.79
Total	46	100	72	100	39	100	69	100

---

[4] This will be subsequently discussed in the ensuing sections.

The table above shows a detailed comparison between MLrs. The results reveal a significant difference between the two groups. MLrs1 differ in the use of the sub-category "Mood derivable" in both their L1 and IL with a difference of (22.58%), whereas MLrs4 with a difference of (51.53%). This being said, one may conclude to the fact that transfer is found in the Mlrs1 in the use of this sub-category as opposed to the MLrs3.

The second sub-strategy is the locution derivable. It is also referred to as the obligation statement. Again, it seems that there are some differences in the use of this strategy by both the groups. MLrs1 differ in the use of the sub-category "Mood derivable" in both their L1 and IL with a difference of (3.51%), while MLrs3 with a difference of (30.61%). Interestingly, these results clearly indicates that there is transfer from L1 into the IL, namely in the performance of the Mlrs. This also demonstrates that transfer decreases as the study level increases.

The last frequently used sub-strategy is the "want statement". Comparing the difference of the performance of the groups in both their L1 and IL, the results yield a significant difference. For instance, MLrs1 differ in the use of this strategy with a difference of (8.19%), whereas Mlrs3 with a difference of (18.68%).

If anything were to be inferred from the results above it will be the fact that there is an impact of L1 on the MLrs" performance in IL. The fact of the matter is that MLrs1 seem to transfer more than their counterpart group. This state of affairs support the research hypotheses that there is evidence of transfer from L1 into IL when EFL Moroccan learners perform request in English as well as that transfer decreases as the study level increases.

IV.3.1.3 Conventionally indirect strategies (CISs)

Table (5) below represents the use of the CIS by MLrs and NSs. The results reveal that the three groups used a variety of CIS. As mentioned before, there are two types of usage which are the amalgamation of conventions of means and conventions of forms. Conventions of means are sentences that are meant to perform an indirect request. Indeed, they are used to question the hearer's ability. Conventions of form, on the other hand, specify the exact wording used for a given indirect request.

Table 10: Rank-ordered Distribution of Sub-strategies of CISs used by NSs and MLrs.

NSs		MLrs1		MLrs3	
Can 24.28%	(17)	Can 43.24%	(32)	Can 47.22%	(34)
Could 14.28%	(10)	Could 21.62%	(16)	Could 33.33%	(24)
Would you mind 14.28%	(10)	Would 18.91%	(14)	Would 9.72%	(7)
I wonder if 8.57%	(6)	Would you mind 6.75%	(5)	I wonder if 2.77%	(2)
Is there any way 8.57%	(6)	I wonder if 2.70%	(2)	May 2.77%	(2)
Do you think 8.57%	(6)	Would it be possible 2.70%	(2)	Shall 1.38%	(1)
Is there any chance 5.71%	(4)	Will 1.35%	(1)	Why Don't you 1.38%	(1)
Would 4.28%	(3)	May 1.35%	(1)	Would you mind 1.38%	(1)
Would it be possible 4.28%	(3)	Do you think 1.35%	(1)		
Would it be alright 2.58%	(2)				
Is it ok if 1.42%	(1)				
Would it be ok 1.42%	(1)				
I was curious if 1.42%	(1)				

The table shows that the sub-strategies "Can" and "Could" are the most frequently used strategies across the three groups. Indeed, once can clearly notice that these sub-strategies are overused by MLrs in the sense that the majority of their CIRs were performed using such

44

strategies. This can be motivated by the fact that MLrs learn these sub-strategies from the very outset of their English learning. Therefore, the overuse of such strategies is somehow expected. Another reason of this overuse is may be their limited linguistic background. The other sub-strategies, however, seem to be undermined. NSs, on the other hand, vary their use of these sub-strategies as opposed to MLrs who were somehow limited in their use.

Bearing in mind what has been said, the result showed clear differences between the three groups in terms of the major requestive strategies used. NSs were found to be the least direct group. Their performance was characterized by the use of CISs. MLrs showed a tendency towards using direct strategies. This tendency may be justified by the fact that there is an impact of MLrs" L1 on their performance in their IL. For the sake of arguments, Kasper (1989) maintains that learners" tendencies towards using given strategies are motivated by learners" preference in L1 and L2. (See also Latif, 2001 for the same view). The least used strategy across the three groups is hints.

In respect to the different sub-strategies employed by the three groups, the results revealed that mood derivable, locution derivable, and want statement were the most frequently used sub-strategies. The findings also indicate that there is an apparent difference between the MLrs in the sense that MLrs1 tended to rely heavily on the mood derivable, while MLrs3 used locution derivable more frequently. There was also found that NSs did not tend to use want statement which implied that there was transfer from L1 into the MLrs" IL. Indeed, the majority of MLrs opted for performing their want statements with the verb "to want" whereas NSs used the verb "to need". This claim was supported by the fact that MLrs tend to use heavily the verb "to want" in their L1. In Abdou (2000), cited in Latif (2001), want statements were realized in Arabic using the verb /brit/. MLrs' limited reliance on "need" might be due to the absence of an equivalent in Moroccan Arabic which has the equivalent function (Latif, 2000: 89).

In terms of CISs, MLrs resorted to overusing the sub-strategies "Can" and "Could". This use may be explained by their limited vocabulary. In fact, NSs showed a rich variety of the use of these sub-strategies at the level of non-conventionally indirect strategies.

IV.3.1.4 Perspectives:

A request can be performed from different perspectives. It can be realized from the viewpoint of the hearer, the speaker, or both participants. To this end, the table below is an attempt to examine the distribution of the perspectives across the three groups.

Table 11: Frequency and percentage of perspectives across the three groups.

Group	Hearer-dominance		Speaker-dominance		Inclusive	
	F	%	F	%	F	%
NSs	44	61.97	24	33.80	3	4.22
MLrs1	65	81.75	15	18.75	–	–
MLrs3	72	91.13	6	7.59	1	1.26

As indicated in the table, "Hearer-dominance" (HD) is the most preferred choice by the three groups. Indeed, MLrs used significantly more HD than NSs with a percentage that ranges from (81%) to (91%), while NSs with a percentage of (61.97%). Another remark one can notice is that MLrs tended to use the Speaker-dominance (SD) as their second choice with a proportion ranged between (18.75%) for MLrs1 and (7.59%) for MLrs3. This inclusive perspective was found to be the least used perspective since it used only by NSs and MLrs3. Mlrs1 could not perform this perspective in their requests.

In order to examine MLrs' performance of perspectives as well as to see any similarities and differences in both their L1 and IL, the table below aims to achieve this goal.

Table 12: Frequency and percentage of perspectives used by MLrs in both their L1 and IL.

Group	Languages	HD		SD		Inclusive		Total	
		F	%	F	%	F	%	F	%
MLrs1	English	65	61.97	15	18.75	–	–	80	100
	M.Arabic	36	75	3	6.25	9	18.75	48	100
MLrs3	English	72	91.13	6	7.59	1	1.26	79	100
	M.Arabic	40	70.17	5	8.77	12	21.05	57	100

As displayed in table (7), it seems that MLrs tend to prefer choosing HD in both their L1 and IL. Furthermore, the results also indicate that the second perspective used is "Inclusive" with a percentage ranged between 18.75% and 21.05%. MLrs did not show this tendency in their IL which means that there is no impact of their L1. Nevertheless, the transfer in the use may be found when one compares MLrs" tendency towards using HD both in their L1 and IL as well as their low performance in using the SD as opposed to their counterpart NSs. This transfer is considered to be negative in the sense that opting for such strategies in their L2 may be perceived as inappropriate when it comes to L2 setting. This results in their pragmalinguistic failure.

Hitherto, the study has attempted to shed light on the major requestive strategies as well as request sub-strategies performed by the three groups, namely NSs and MLrs In terms of directness preference, the results showed that NSs were the least direct group, followed by MLrs1 and then MLrs3. The findings also revealed that MLrs showed a similar tendency towards performing their requests in direct strategies in both their L1 and IL as opposed to NSs. This implies that there is transfer from L1 into IL when MLrs perform request in English. This seems to support the first research hypothesis which is „There is evidence of pragmatic transfer in the English requests produced by Moroccan learners of English". Interestingly enough, the results also indicated that MLrs1 seemed to transfer more than their counterpart group MLrs3 which also appears to support the second research hypothesis that is Pragmatic transfer decreases as the study level increases.

At the level of perspectives, to recapitulate, the results yielded some similarities between MLrs" performance in L1 and IL. They both seemed to rely heavily on HD perspective as well as their low tendency towards SD perspectives. These findings also support Latif (2001) who maintained that there is negative transfer by MLrs in their performance of HD perspective in the sense that their use outperformed that of NSs. He also suggested that their preference for HD may be explained by the scarcity if not the lack of SD phrased in their L1 (Moroccan Arabic). In order to move this line of results further, it important to examine the issue of transfer from a sociopragmatic level.

IV.4 Sociopragmatic Analysis

Sociopragmatics is defined as the interface of linguistic action and social structure. More specifically, it demonstrates the effect of such limitation as social status, social distance and degree of imposition on the choice of linguistic realization of a particular communicative acts and strategies. For this fact, transfer will be examined in terms of each situation in order to see the influence of the social variable on the use of the requesting strategies across the three groups.

IV.4.1 Directness

The table below provides a rigorous view at the different situations so as to see how these strategies were used across the groups both in their L1 and IL.

Table 13: Frequency and percentage of perspectives used by MLrs in both their L1 and IL.

Situations	Strategies	NSs	MLrs1		MLrs 3	
			English	M.Arabic	English	M.Arabic
1	1	–	35.30%	68.75%	11.11%	50%
	2	100%	64.70%	31.25%	83.33%	45.83%
	3	–	–	–	5.55%	8.33%
2	1	85.71%	52.63%	76.92%	71.42%	83.34%
	2	14.28%	42.10%	7.69%	19.04%	8.33%
	3	14.28%	5.26%	15.38%	9.52%	8.33%
3	1	18.75%	84.22%	82.60%	65.53%	88.24%
	2	50%	15.78%	–	30.43%	5.88%
	3	31.25%	–	17.39%	13.04%	5.88%
4	1	6.25%	5.26%	33.34%	15.78%	33.35%
	2	93.75%	89.48%	66.66%	78.94%	47.61%
	3	–	5.26%	–	5.28%	19.04%
5	1	12.50%	10%	28.57%	50%	41.17%
	2	81.25%	90%	66.66%	44.44%	52.95%
	3	6.25%	–	4.76%	5.56%	5.88%
6	1	6.68%	38.88%	65%	15%	47.05%
	2	86.66%	61.12%	35%	65%	41.17%
	3	6.66%	–	–	–	11.47%
7	1	–	6.66%	47.05%	5%	46.66%
	2	100%	93.34%	52.95%	95%	53.34%
	3	–	–	–	–	–
	1:Direct Strategies		2:CIRs		3: Hints	

Situation 1: Borrowing (=P, +D, -IM, B)[5] In this situation, the power status between the speaker and the hearer is described as equal; NSs performed all their request goal in CISs. Mlrs, on the other hand, varied their request in both their L1 and IL. MLrs3 seemed to be the least direct group with a percentage of (83.33%), while MLrs1 (64.70%). In fact, this situation provides a vivid picture of the negative transfer that L1 exerts on MLrs. This influence is explained by their preference of using direct strategies in this situation.

Situation 2: Parking (+P, -D, +IM, A) In this situation, the speaker is in a position of power who is asking a driver to move his/her car from a no-parking area. The interlocutors are not familiar with each other, and the request goal is asking for a right/duty. The sociopragmatic parameters of this situation necessitate a high imposition request. Therefore, a higher degree of directness is expected. As indicated in the table, the three groups were equally footed in terms of their use of direct strategies. This may be justified by the fact the three groups perceived the situation as similar in both the cultures insofar as MLrs also perform the request of this situation in direct strategies in their L1. Hence, this may be considered as a positive transfer.

Situation 3: Kitchen (=P, +D, -IM, A) This situation contains somehow the same socio-opragmatic variables as situation 1 except for that the speaker is asking for a right which is to commit the hearer to clean the kitchen. This situation is also characterized by the lack of social distance, combined with the low rate of imposition. The results indicated that MLrs1 appeared to be the most direct group with a percentage of (84.22%). Their performance in their IL was quite the same in their L1 with a percentage of (82.60%). Whereas MLrs3 with a (65.53%) and (88.24%) in their L1. NSs, on the other hand, seemed to be the least direct group in the sense that (50%) of their requests were performed in CISs. In this situation academic level proved to be a key factor in MLrs" performance. MLrs1 were more influenced by their L1.

Situation 4: Student to Professor (-P, +D, +IM, B) This situation is concerned with a student who is asking his professor to postpone the exam next week. The hearer is supposed to be in a superior position as compared to the student. Their relationship is considered to be familiar (although it could be argued that the interlocutors do not have a personal relationship; see Latif 2001). This scenario resulted that NS were the least direct group with a percentage of (93.75%), followed by MLrs1 (89.48%), and then MLrs3 (78.94%). As a matter of fact,

---

[5] It should be pointed that some of the subjects failed to understand some of the situations; hence their sequences were discarded.

MLrs, again, showed a tendency towards performing a great number of their requests in direct strategies. Indeed, this tendency, as one may clearly notice when one compares their performance in L1 and IL, is similar in their L1. Accordingly, transfer is quite clear in this situation.

Situation 5: Permission (-P, +D, +IM, C) In this situation, the speaker wants to ask his/her father for a permission to go to a party organized by friends. The sociopragmatic parameters of this situation require a low imposition request in the sense that both the interlocutors are familiar. However, the speaker is supposed to be in an inferior status. Thus, the use of politeness strategies is expected. This was the case for MLrs who performed (90%) of their requests in CISs, followed by NSs (81.25%). MLrs3, on other hand, appeared to be extremely influenced by their L1 in the sense they showed an overwhelming tendency towards the use of direct strategies in both their L1 and IL. In this situation and in the previous academic do not seem to play key role in the use of the strategies.

Situation 6: (+P, +D, +IM, A) In this situation, the speaker is in a position of power who is asking his/her secretary to work overtime. This situation is also characterized by the lack of social distance, combined with the high rate of imposition in the sense that the manager is asking for extratime. As shown in the table above, NSs tended to perform a high rate of their requests in CISs (86.66%). In a similar way, MLrs seemed to opt for CISs with a percentage of that ranged from (61.12%) to (65%), while a number of their strategies were used in direct strategies. However, the difference between NSs and MLrs in this situation is quite clear.

Situation 7: (=P, -D, +IM, B) The last situation involves someone who wants a book in the library, but it happens that book is on the top shelf; therefore, the speaker intents to ask someone else to get it for him. The power status between the speaker and the unknown interlocutor is described as equal, but the speaker is faced with the added difficulty of asking the hearer in the sense that they are both unfamiliar with each other. Thus, the speaker will seek for positive politeness strategies. The results of this scenario indicated that the three groups perceived the situation equally, for they all opted for performing their requests in CISs. Therefore, transfer is considered to be positive.

This being the case, the results, as one may conclude, presented a number of differences between the groups in terms of each situation. The three groups varied their requestive strategies across the situation. MLrs appeared to be influenced by their L1 norms. Indeed, they showed a quite clear tendency towards using direct strategies in almost all the situations in their L1. This also affected their performance in their IL. However, results also revealed some similarities between MLrs and NSs. For example, in situation (2) where a high imposition request and a higher degree of directness is expected, the three groups performed their requests in the same way opting for direct strategies. It should also be pointed that transfer was found in both the groups, namely in situation (3) where MLrs opted for using direct strategies in both their L1 and IL. This transfer is explained by virtue of their perception of some of the situation that was different from NSs" perception and performance Noteworthy is that academic level did not seem to play a major role in pragmatic situation for in some situations MLrs1 seemed to be similar to NSs as opposed to MLrs3 who were apparently influenced more than their counterpart by their L1 norms.

IV.4.2 Perspectives

The table below concerned with presenting a distribution of perspectives by NSs and MLrs by situation so as to see how the use of perspectives vary according to the sociopragmatic factors present in a given situation

Table 14: Frequencies of perspectives across the three groups by situations.

Situations	Groups		Hearer-dominance	Speaker-dominance	Inclusive
1	1	English	5	10	0
	2	English	14	2	0
		M.Arabic	9	0	0
	3	English	15	1	0
		M.Arabic	12	0	0
2	1	English	1	0	0
	2	English	8	0	0
		M.Arabic	0	0	0
	3	English	3	0	0
		M.Arabic	0	0	0
3	1	English	9	0	0
	2	English	2	0	0
		M.Arabic	0	0	0
	3	English	7	0	0
		M.Arabic	0	0	0

4	1	English	2	5	3
	2	English	15	1	0
		M.Arabic	6	0	9
	3	English	15	0	1
		M.Arabic	3	0	12
5	1	English	1	10	0
	2	English	3	12	0
		M.Arabic	7	2	0
	3	English	7	5	0
		M.Arabic	5	5	0
6	1	English	12	0	0
	2	English	10	0	0
		M.Arabic	3	1	0
	3	English	6	0	0
		M.Arabic	7	0	0
7	1	English	13	0	0
	2	English	16	0	0
		M.Arabic	11	0	0
	3	English	18	0	0
		M.Arabic	12	0	0

1: NSs   2:MLrs1   3:MLrs3

As displayed in table above, it seems that MLrs tend to prefer choosing HD in both their L1 and IL whereas NSs" requests contain SD perspective. However, this tendency is not true in situation (7) and (6). To recapitulate, these two situations are characterized by a high rate of imposition as well as the use of positive politeness strategies, for this request constitutes a face-threatening act. On the contrary, where the power status between the speaker and the hearer is equal, NSs tend to realize their requests mostly through the use of the SD perspective. MLrs realize virtually all their requests through the use of HD. save for situation 5. The influence of L1 on IL appears clearly in situation 1 and 4 where MLrs performed their requests using HD as opposed to NSs.

A further examination reveals that academic level does again play a major role in pragmatic transfer. In other words, the results showed more similarities than differences between the level groups. Indeed, they both seem to be influenced by their L1 setting, thereby transferring this setting into their IL which in turn may result in pragmatic failure when it comes to L1 norms.

All things considered, the results provide evidence supporting the first research hypothesis the present study has formulated that there is evidence of pragmatic transfer in the English requests produced by Moroccan learners of English. This transfer is exerted by MLrs" L1. Transfer was found in two levels: 1) Pragmalinguistic level that is in the use strategies and perspectives and 2) The sociopragmatic level which aimed at examining the impact of the situational variables such as social distance, power relation, and the degree of imposition on the performance of the speech act of request. A detailed analysis showed that MLrs and NSs differ in the use of these strategies. Besides, results also revealed that MLrs1 and MLrs are different in terms of the choice of directness and requestive strategies. However, the findings also indicate that academic level does not play a major role in pragmatic ability. In fact, a number of studies undertaken in the field of interlanguage and cross-cultural pragmatics have provided evidence on that the fact that L2 learners' L1 pragmatic knowledge affect their perception and production of pragmatic performance in L2. (Ellis, 1994; Kasper & Dahl, 1991; Kasper & Rose, 1999; Benbarka, 2002, among so many others).

IV.5 Conclusion

This chapter was concerned with presenting a detailed analysis and a discussion of the data gathered. This chapter has attempted to shed light on the various strategies used by NSs and MLrs. Indeed, the use of these strategies was analyzed at two levels: pragmalinguistic and sociopragmatic level by means of frequencies and percentages. In the coming chapter, a summary of the objectives and results will be introduced, along with drawing some research implications and pedagogical applications.

General Conclusion

V.1 Summary of the objectives

This study purported to investigate the issue of pragmatic transfer from L1 into the interlanguage of Moroccan learners of English, namely when they make requests in English. More specifically, this study sought to compare the average frequencies of direct and indirect strategies used by both native Moroccan English as a foreign language learners and native speakers of English. Finally, this study has further attempted to explore whether transfer decreases as the study level increased, the case of the Moroccan EFL university learners: The first and the third level of university.

V.2 Summary of the Methodology

A number of fifty six subjects took part in the present study. They were divided into two groups. The first group involved the Moroccan learners of English who in turn bifurcated into two groups of academic level: Second Year (N=20) and Third year (N=20). The subjects in the second group were 20 native speakers of English. In order to answer the research questions addressed by this study, the DCT was adopted. This DCT provided the subject with a number of seven situations in which different situations were controlled, namely social distance, power relation, and the degree of imposition. A Moroccan Arabic DCT was also used in order to examine how Moroccan students perform requests in their mother tongues. In fact, the whole seven situations were identical to that of English. In analyzing the data, a number of techniques were adopted, namely the frequency and percentage analyses whereby the different strategies were described across the groups.

V.3 Summary of the Results

The findings in this study seem to strongly confirm the first research hypothesis:

H1: There is evidence of pragmatic transfer in the English requests produced by Moroccan learners of English.

Transfer was found in two levels: 1) Pragmalinguistic level that is in the use strategies and perspectives and 2) The sociopragmatic level which aimed at examining the impact of the situational variables such as social distance, power relation, and the degree of imposition on the performance of the speech act of request. A detailed analysis showed that MLrs and NSs differ in the use of these strategies. Besides, results also revealed that MLrs1 and MLrs3 are different in terms of the choice of directness and requestive strategies. However, the findings also indicated that academic level does not play a significant role in pragmatic ability. For this fact, the second research hypothesis was rejected in favor of the null hypothesis drawing the conclusion that pragmatic transfer is not related to academic level.

V.4 Limitation of the study

Given time constraints, there are a number of limitations that need to be mentioned. To start with, this study made use of only one major instrument that is the DCT. As stated before, this instrument has many drawbacks. Hence, it was assumed that many participants may not respond as spontaneously as in natural situation because they have time to think and prepare to the situations. Furthermore, the number of subjects is not large so as to one can generalize the results. Another limitation is that of NSs who were difficult to find. Therefore, the number of NSs subjects was less than that of MLrs. Finally, this study analyzed the data only by means of frequencies and percentages and, therefore, not allowing for inferential statistics. In short, the present study is only a phase towards further research that would take into account the limitation presented above.

V.5 Research Implications

There are many implications for future research the present study suggests. Firstly, there is a need to study pragmatic transfer in terms of variables such as age and gender in order to see whether age affects the performance of request and, indeed, to see the average frequencies of direct and indirect strategies used by both males and females. Second, future study should use more than one instrument. Instruments that focus on the use of requests in natural settings. This research also calls to involve Baccalaureate students in order to see whether academic level is true a key factor in the performance of request or not.

V.6 Pedagogical Implications

Pragmatic competence, as has been seen, plays a major role in the communicative failure of a number of non-native speakers" learners. For this reason, foreign language instructors and teachers have to include in their curriculum teaching pragmatic competence so as to raise both learners" pragmalinguistic and sociopragmatic awareness of the target language they intend to acquire and, more precisely, the target speech acts (Kasper & Rose, 2001). Furthermore, pragmatic competence ought to be taught at schools so that non-native learners may be exposed to and familiar with the target language norms and conventions at an early age. In this respect, Cook (2001) suggests that the raising of instructors" pragmatic, sociolinguistic and discoursal knowledge of the target language and culture is very important, for it is the key to effective pragmatic language teaching.

V.7 Conclusion

The focus of this chapter has been to offer a conclusion of the main points discussed in this study. The chapter has brought into focus a summary of the main objectives and a description of the methodology adopted; it provided a summary of the results and the limitations of the current study. Indeed, attention has also been drawn to the major pedagogical implications syllabus designers that should take into consideration in their textbooks.

References

Abdou, M. 1999. *Proficiency Level in English and Previous Linguistic Background as Constraints on Pragmatic Competence in EFL in Morocco: The case of Request*. Unpublished DESA Dissertation, Faculty of Education. Mohamed V, Souissi, Rabat.

Achiba, M. 2003. *Learning to Request in Second Language: A study of Child Interlanguage Pragmatics*. Printed and bound in Great Britain by the Cromwell Press Ltd.

Austin, J. 1962. *How to Do Things with Words*. Oxford: Oxford University Press.

Bachman, L. F. 1990. *Fundamental Considerations in Language Testing*. Oxford. Oxford, University press.

Barron, A. 2003. *Acquisition in Interlanguage Pragmatics: Learning how to Do things with Words in a Study Abroad Context*. Amsterdam: Benjamins.

Becker, J. 1982. "Children's Strategic Use of Requests to Mark and Manipulate Social Status". In S. Kuczaj II (ed.) *Language Development: Language, Thought and Culture* (pp. 1–35). Hillsdale, NJ: Lawrence Erlbaum.

Beebe, L. and Takahashi, T. 1989. "Variation in Interlanguage Speech Act Realization". In S. Gass, C. Madden, D. Preston and L. Selinker (eds) *Variation in Second Language Acquisition: Discourse and Pragmatics* (pp. 103–25). Clevedon: Multilingual Matters.

Benbarka, L. 2002. *Pragmatic Transfer in EFL Moroccan Learners Apologies*. Unpublished DESA dissertation, Faculty of Education. Mohamed V, Souissi. Rabat.

Blum-Kulka, S. 1982. "Learning to Say what You Mean in a Second Language: A study of the Speech Act Performance of Learners of Hebrew as a Second Language". *Applied Linguistics* 3, 29–59.

Blum-Kulka, S. 1985. "Modifiers as Indicating Devices: The Case of Requests". Paper presented at *the Conference on Cognitive Aspects of the Utterance, Tel Aviv*.

Blum-Kulka, S. 1989. "Playing it Safe: The Role of Conventionality in Indirectness". In S. Blum-Kulka, J. House and G. Kasper (eds) *Cross-cultural Pragmatics: Requests and Apologies* (pp. 37–70). Norwood, NJ: Ablex.

Blum-Kulka, S. 1991. "Interlanguage Pragmatics: the Case of Requests". In Philipson, R., Kellerman, E., Selinker, L., Sharwood-smith, M., and Swain, M. (Eds.). *Foreign/ Second Language Pedagogy Research* (pp.255-272). Multilingual Matters.

Blum-Kulka, S. and House, J. 1989. "Cross-cultural and Situational Variation in Requesting Behavior". In S. Blum-Kulka, J. House and G. Kasper (Eds) *Cross-cultural Pragmatics: Requests and Apologies* (pp. 123–54). Norwood, NJ: Ablex.

Blum-Kulka, S., House, J. and Kasper, G. (Eds). 1989a. *Cross-cultural Pragmatics: Requests and Apologies*. Norwood, NJ: Ablex.

Blum-Kulka, S. and Levinson, E.A. 1983. "Universals of Lexical simplification". In Faerch, C. and Kasper, G, G. (Eds) *Strategies in Interlanguage Communication*. London. Longman.

Bou-Franch, P. 1998. "On Pragmatic Transfer". SELL: *Studies in English Language and Linguistics*, 0, 5-20.

Brown, P. and Levinson, S. 1978, 1987. *Politeness: Some Universals in Language Usage*. Cambridge: Cambridge University Press.

Canal, M. 1983. "From Communicative Competence to Communicative Language Pedagogy". In Richards, J. C. and Schimdit, R. W (Eds). *Language and communication*. Longman. London.

Chomsky, N. 1965. *Aspects of the Theory of Syntax*. Cambridge: MIT Press.

Clark, H. and Schunk, D. 1980. "Polite Responses to Polite Requests". *Cognition* 8, 111–43.

Cook, H. 2001. "Why Can't Students of JFL Distinguish Polite from Impolite Speech Styles?". In K. Rose and G. Kasper (eds) *Pragmatics in Language Teaching* (pp. 80–102). Cambridge: Cambridge University Press.

Ellis, R. 1994. *The Study of Second Language Acquisition*. Oxford: Oxford University Press.

Fraser, B. 1978. "Acquiring Social Competence in a Second Language". *RELC Journal*, 9(2), 1–21.

Grice, H. P. 1975. "Logic and Conversation". In P. Cole & J. L. Morgan (Eds.), *Syntax and Semantics Volume 3: Speech Acts* (pp. 41–58). London: Academic Press.

Holtgraves, T. 1986. "Language Structure in Social Interaction: Perceptions of Direct and Indirect Speech Acts and Interactions who Use them". *Journal of Personality and Social Psychology* 305 14.

House, J. 1989. "Politeness in English and German: The functions of Please and Bitte". In S. Blum Kulka, J. House & G. Kasper (Eds.), *Cross-cultural pragmatics: Requests and Apologies* (pp. 96–122). Norwood, NJ: Ablex.

Hymes, D. H. 1972. On Communicative Competence. In J. B. Pride & J. Holmes (Eds.), Sociolinguistics (pp. 269–293). Harmondsworth: Penguin.

Kasper, G. 1997. "Can Pragmatic Competence be Taught?" (NFLRC Net Work No. 6.) Honolulu: University of Hawaii at Manoa, Second Language Teaching & Curriculum Center.

Kasper, G. 1998. "Communication Strategies: Modality Reduction". *Interlanguage Studies Bulletin*, 4/2, 266-283. Utrecht. NJ: Ablex.

Kasper, G. and Dahl, M. 1991. "Research Methods in Interlanguage Pragmatics". *Studies in Second Language Acquisition* 13, 215-47.

Kasper, G. and Rose, K. 1999. "Pragmatics and SLA". *Annual Review of Applied Linguistics* 19, 81–104.

Kasper, G. and Schmidt, R. 1996. "Developmental Issues in Interlanguage Pragmatics". *Studies in Second Language Acquisition* 18, 149–69.

Latif, H. 2001. *A Sociopragmatic study of EFL Moroccan Learners' Requests*. Unpublished DESA dissertation, Faculty of Education. Mohamed V, Souissi, Rabat.

Leech, G. 1983. *Principles of Pragmatics*. London: Longman.

Levinson, S. C. 1983. *Pragmatics*. Cambridge: Cambridge University Press.

Lin, M. 2008. "Pragmatic Failure in Intercultural Communication and English Teaching in China". *China Media Research*, 4(3), 43-52.

Oldin, T. 1989. *Language Transfer*. Cambridge: Cambridge University Press.

Olshtain, E., & Blum-Kulka, S. 1985. "Degree of Approximation: Nonnative Reactions to Native Speech Act Behaviour". In S. M. Gass & C. G. Madden (Eds.), *Input in Second Language Acquisition* (pp. 303–325). Rowley: Newbury House.

Schimdit, R. W. & Richards, J. C. 1980. "Speech Acts and Second Language Learning". *Applied Linguistics*, 1/2, 129-157.

Searle, J. 1969. *Speech Acts: An Essay in the Philosophy of Language*. Cambridge: Cambridge University Press.

Searle, J. 1975. "Indirect Speech Acts". In P. Cole and J. Morgan (eds) *Syntax and Semantics 3: Speech Acts* (pp. 59–82). New York: Academic Press.

Searle, J. 1976. "A Classification of Illocutionary Acts". *Language in Society* 5, 1–23.

Sharwood-Smith, M. & Kellerman, E. 1986. "Cross-Linguistic Influence in Second Language Acquisition: An Introduction". In E. Kellerman & M. Sharwood-Smith (eds) *Cross-Linguistic Influence in Second Language Acquisition*, New York: Pergamon, 1-9.

Thomas, J. 1983. "Cross-cultural Pragmatic Failure". *Applied Linguistics* 4, 91–112.

Weizman, E. 1989. "Requestive Hints". In S. Blum-Kulka, J. House and G. Kasper (eds) *Cross-cultural Pragmatics: Requests and Apologies* (pp. 71–95). Norwood, NJ: Ablex.

Weizman, E. 1993. "Interlanguage Requestive Hints". In G. Kasper and S. Blum-Kulka (eds) *Interlanguage Pragmatics* (pp. 123–37). New York: Oxford.